This ~~book~~ Experiment belongs to:

_____

_____

The Story Behind the Title...

My grandmother was a masterful cook. She loved searching for new recipes and making the best homemade meals on the planet (in my opinion).

When she got older, cooking became too difficult for her due to the use of a walker and her inability to stand for long periods. My mother moved in with her to care for her and let's just say that she did not share that same enthusiasm for the kitchen. My mother stuck to simple staples in her menu or they went out to eat.

One night my mother made spaghetti with homemade meat sauce, which took her most of the day and when they finished eating dinner, my mother asked how it was, to which my grandmother replied, "I ate it. It didn't kill me".

This has become the favorite quote in our family after meals and we always think of her and giggle.

Table of Contents

3

Table of Contents

Important Phone Numbers

Fire Department: _____

Poison Control: _____

Ambulance: _____

Hospital: _____

Friend Who Bought
This Book for you: _____

Recipe: _____

Source: _____
(who to blame)

| Servings | Prep Time (triple this) | Cooking Time (will probably take longer) | Temperature |

INGREDIENTS:

_____
_____
_____
_____
_____
_____
_____
_____
_____
_____
_____
_____
_____
_____
_____
_____
_____
_____
_____
_____
_____
_____
_____
_____
_____
_____
_____

Notes/Substitutions:

_____
_____
_____
_____

DiRectioNS: (if you choose to follow them)

(blank lined space)

About My Masterpiece:

(blank lined space)

(photographic evidence)

Recipe: _____

Source: _____
(who to blame)

_____ _____ _____ _____
Servings   Prep Time   Cooking Time   Temperature
            (triple this) (will probably take longer)

INGREDIENTS:

_____
_____
_____
_____
_____
_____
_____
_____
_____
_____
_____
_____
_____
_____
_____
_____
_____
_____
_____
_____
_____
_____
_____
_____
_____
_____

Notes/Substitutions:
_____
_____
_____
_____

DiRectioNS: (if you choose to follow them)

_____
_____
_____
_____
_____
_____
_____
_____
_____
_____
_____
_____
_____
_____
_____
_____

About My MasteRpiece:

_____
_____
_____
_____

(photogRaphic evidence)

Recipe: _____

Source: _____
(who to blame)

_____ _____ _____ _____
Servings   Prep Time   Cooking Time   Temperature
              (triple this) (will probably take longer)

INGREDIENTS:

_____
_____
_____
_____
_____
_____
_____
_____
_____
_____
_____
_____
_____
_____
_____
_____
_____
_____
_____
_____
_____
_____
_____
_____
_____

Notes/Substitutions:

_____
_____
_____

DiReCTioNS: (if you choose to follow them)

About My MasterPiece:

(photographic evidence)

Recipe: _____

Source: _____
(who to blame)

_____ _____ _____ _____
Servings   Prep Time   Cooking Time   Temperature
                   (triple this)   (will probably take longer)

INGREDIENTS:

_____
_____
_____
_____
_____
_____
_____
_____
_____
_____
_____
_____
_____
_____
_____
_____
_____
_____
_____
_____
_____
_____
_____
_____
_____
_____
_____

Notes/Substitutions:

_____
_____
_____
_____

DiRectioNS: (if you choose to follow them)

_____
_____
_____
_____
_____
_____
_____
_____
_____
_____
_____
_____
_____
_____
_____

About My Masterpiece:

_____
_____
_____

(photographic evidence)

Recipe: _____

Source: _____
(who to blame)

| Servings | Prep Time (triple this) | Cooking Time (will probably take longer) | Temperature |

INGReDieNTS:

_____
_____
_____
_____
_____
_____
_____
_____
_____
_____
_____
_____
_____
_____
_____
_____
_____
_____
_____
_____
_____
_____
_____
_____
_____

Notes/Substitutions:

_____
_____
_____

DirectioNS: (if you choose to follow them)

About My Masterpiece:

(photographic evidence)

Recipe: _____

Source: _____
(who to blame)

_____	_____	_____	_____
Servings	Prep Time	Cooking Time	Temperature
	(triple this)	(will probably take longer)	

INGREDIENTS:

_____
_____
_____
_____
_____
_____
_____
_____
_____
_____
_____
_____
_____
_____
_____
_____
_____
_____
_____
_____
_____
_____
_____
_____
_____
_____
_____

Notes/Substitutions:
_____
_____
_____
_____

DiRectioNS: (if you choose to follow them)

_____
_____
_____
_____
_____
_____
_____
_____
_____
_____
_____
_____
_____
_____
_____

About My MasteRpiece:

_____
_____
_____

(photoGRaphic evidence)

Recipe: _____

Source: _____
(who to blame)

_____ _____ _____ _____
Servings   Prep Time   Cooking Time   Temperature
              (triple this) (will probably take longer)

INGRedients:

_____
_____
_____
_____
_____
_____
_____
_____
_____
_____
_____
_____
_____
_____
_____
_____
_____
_____
_____
_____
_____
_____
_____
_____
_____

Notes/Substitutions:

_____
_____
_____
_____

DiRectioNS: (if you choose to follow them)

About My MasteRpiece:

(photographic evidence)

Recipe: _____

Source: _____
(who to blame)

_____ _____ _____ _____
Servings   Prep Time   Cooking Time   Temperature
            (triple this) (will probably take longer)

INGREDIENTS:

_____
_____
_____
_____
_____
_____
_____
_____
_____
_____
_____
_____
_____
_____
_____
_____
_____
_____
_____
_____
_____
_____
_____
_____

Notes/Substitutions:
_____
_____
_____

DiRectioNS: (if you choose to follow them)

About My MasterPiece:

(photographic evidence)

Recipe: _____

Source: _____
(who to blame)

Servings	Prep Time (triple this)	Cooking Time (will probably take longer)	Temperature

INGREDIENTS:

_____
_____
_____
_____
_____
_____
_____
_____
_____
_____
_____
_____
_____
_____
_____
_____
_____
_____
_____
_____
_____
_____
_____
_____
_____
_____
_____
_____
_____

Notes/Substitutions:

_____
_____
_____
_____

DiRectioNS: (if you choose to follow them)

About My MasteRpiece:

(photographic evidence)

Recipe: _____

Source: _____
(who to blame)

_____ _____ _____ _____
Servings   Prep Time   Cooking Time   Temperature
            (triple this) (will probably take longer)

INGREDIENTS:

Notes/Substitutions:

DIRECTIONS: (if you choose to follow them)

About My Masterpiece:

(photographic evidence)

Recipe: _____

Source: _____
(who to blame)

_____   _____   _____   _____
Servings   Prep Time   Cooking Time   Temperature
             (triple this) (will probably take longer)

INGredients:

_____
_____
_____
_____
_____
_____
_____
_____
_____
_____
_____
_____
_____
_____
_____
_____
_____
_____
_____
_____
_____
_____
_____
_____
_____
_____
_____
_____

Notes/Substitutions:

_____
_____
_____
_____

Directions: (if you choose to follow them)

About My Masterpiece:

(photographic evidence)

Recipe: _____

Source: _____
(who to blame)

_____ _____ _____ _____
Servings   Prep Time   Cooking Time   Temperature
           (triple this)   (will probably take longer)

INGREDIENTS:

_____
_____
_____
_____
_____
_____
_____
_____
_____
_____
_____
_____
_____
_____
_____
_____
_____
_____
_____
_____
_____
_____
_____
_____
_____
_____
_____
_____

Notes/Substitutions:

_____
_____
_____
_____

DIRECTIONS: (if you choose to follow them)

About My Masterpiece:

(photographic evidence)

Recipe: _____

Source: _____
(who to blame)

_____ _____ _____ _____
Servings   Prep Time   Cooking Time   Temperature
              (triple this) (will probably take longer)

INGREDIENTS:

_____
_____
_____
_____
_____
_____
_____
_____
_____
_____
_____
_____
_____
_____
_____
_____
_____
_____
_____
_____
_____
_____
_____
_____

Notes/Substitutions:
_____
_____
_____

DIRECTIONS: (if you choose to follow them)

About My Masterpiece:

(photographic evidence)

Recipe: _____

Source: _____
(who to blame)

Servings	Prep Time	Cooking Time	Temperature
_____	_____ (triple this)	_____ (will probably take longer)	_____

INGREDIENTS:

_____
_____
_____
_____
_____
_____
_____
_____
_____
_____
_____
_____
_____
_____
_____
_____
_____
_____
_____
_____
_____
_____
_____
_____
_____
_____
_____
_____

Notes/Substitutions:

_____
_____
_____
_____

DiRectioNS: (if you choose to follow them)

_____
_____
_____
_____
_____
_____
_____
_____
_____
_____
_____
_____
_____
_____

About My Masterpiece:

_____
_____
_____

(photographic evidence)

Recipe: _____

Source: _____
(who to blame)

| Servings | Prep Time (triple this) | Cooking Time (will probably take longer) | Temperature |

INGREDIENTS:

_____
_____
_____
_____
_____
_____
_____
_____
_____
_____
_____
_____
_____
_____
_____
_____
_____
_____
_____
_____
_____
_____
_____
_____
_____

Notes/Substitutions:

_____
_____
_____

Directions: (if you choose to follow them)

About My Masterpiece:

(photographic evidence)

Recipe: _____

Source: _____
(who to blame)

_____   _____   _____   _____
Servings   Prep Time   Cooking Time   Temperature
                        (triple this)   (will probably take longer)

INGREDIENTS:

_____
_____
_____
_____
_____
_____
_____
_____
_____
_____
_____
_____
_____
_____
_____
_____
_____
_____
_____
_____
_____
_____
_____
_____
_____
_____
_____
_____
_____
_____

Notes/Substitutions:

_____
_____
_____
_____

DiRectioNS: (if you choose to follow them)

About My MasteRpiece:

(photographic evidence)

Recipe: _____

Source: _____
(who to blame)

Servings	Prep Time	Cooking Time	Temperature
	(triple this)	(will probably take longer)	

INGREDIENTS:

_____

_____

_____

_____

_____

_____

_____

_____

_____

_____

_____

_____

_____

_____

_____

_____

_____

_____

_____

_____

_____

_____

_____

_____

_____

Notes/Substitutions:

_____

_____

_____

_____

DiRections: (if you choose to follow them)

About My Masterpiece:

(photographic evidence)

Recipe: _____

Source: _____
(who to blame)

Servings	Prep Time	Cooking Time	Temperature
	(triple this)	(will probably take longer)	

INGReDieNTS:

_____
_____
_____
_____
_____
_____
_____
_____
_____
_____
_____
_____
_____
_____
_____
_____
_____
_____
_____
_____
_____
_____
_____
_____
_____
_____
_____
_____

Notes/Substitutions:

_____
_____
_____
_____

DiRectioNS: (if you choose to follow them)

About My MasterPiece:

(photographic evidence)

Recipe: _____

Source: _____
(who to blame)

| Servings | Prep Time (triple this) | Cooking Time (will probably take longer) | Temperature |

INGREDIENTS:

_____
_____
_____
_____
_____
_____
_____
_____
_____
_____
_____
_____
_____
_____
_____
_____
_____
_____
_____
_____
_____
_____
_____
_____
_____

Notes/Substitutions:

_____
_____
_____

DiRectioNs: (if you choose to follow them)

About My Masterpiece:

(photographic evidence)

43

Recipe: _____

Source: _____
(who to blame)

_____ _____ _____ _____
Servings   Prep Time   Cooking Time   Temperature
              (triple this) (will probably take longer)

INGREDIENTS:

_____
_____
_____
_____
_____
_____
_____
_____
_____
_____
_____
_____
_____
_____
_____
_____
_____
_____
_____
_____
_____
_____
_____
_____
_____
_____
_____
_____

Notes/Substitutions:

_____
_____
_____
_____

Directions: (if you choose to follow them)

About My Masterpiece:

(photographic evidence)

45

Recipe: _____

Source: _____
(who to blame)

_____ | _____ | _____ | _____
Servings | Prep Time | Cooking Time | Temperature
| (triple this) | (will probably take longer) |

INGReDiENts:

_____
_____
_____
_____
_____
_____
_____
_____
_____
_____
_____
_____
_____
_____
_____
_____
_____
_____
_____
_____
_____
_____
_____
_____
_____
_____
_____

Notes/Substitutions:

_____
_____
_____

DIRECTIONS: (if you choose to follow them)

About My Masterpiece:

(photographic evidence)

Recipe: _____

Source: _____
(who to blame)

_____ | _____ | _____ | _____
Servings | Prep Time | Cooking Time | Temperature
| (triple this) | (will probably take longer) |

INGREDIENTS:

_____

_____

_____

_____

_____

_____

_____

_____

_____

_____

_____

_____

_____

_____

_____

_____

_____

_____

_____

_____

_____

_____

_____

_____

_____

_____

_____

Notes/Substitutions:

_____

_____

_____

Directions: (if you choose to follow them)

About My Masterpiece:

(photographic evidence)

Recipe: _____

Source: _____
(who to blame)

_____   _____   _____   _____
Servings   Prep Time   Cooking Time   Temperature
            (triple this)   (will probably take longer)

INGREDIENTS:

_____
_____
_____
_____
_____
_____
_____
_____
_____
_____
_____
_____
_____
_____
_____
_____
_____
_____
_____
_____
_____
_____
_____
_____
_____

Notes/Substitutions:

_____
_____
_____

DiRectioNs: (if you choose to follow them)

_____

_____

_____

_____

_____

_____

_____

_____

_____

_____

_____

_____

_____

_____

_____

_____

About My Masterpiece:

_____

_____

_____

_____

(photographic evidence)

Recipe: _____

Source: _____
(who to blame)

| _____ | _____ | _____ | _____ |
| Servings | Prep Time (triple this) | Cooking Time (will probably take longer) | Temperature |

INGReDieNts:

_____
_____
_____
_____
_____
_____
_____
_____
_____
_____
_____
_____
_____
_____
_____
_____
_____
_____
_____
_____
_____
_____
_____
_____
_____
_____
_____

Notes/Substitutions:

_____
_____
_____
_____

Directions: (if you choose to follow them)

About My Masterpiece:

(photographic evidence)

Recipe: _____

Source: _____
(who to blame)

_____ _____ _____ _____
Servings   Prep Time   Cooking Time   Temperature
                           (triple this)   (will probably take longer)

INGREDIENTS:

_____

_____

_____

_____

_____

_____

_____

_____

_____

_____

_____

_____

_____

_____

_____

_____

_____

_____

_____

_____

_____

_____

_____

Notes/Substitutions:

_____

_____

_____

DiReCtioNS: (if you choose to follow them)

About My MasterPiece:

(photographic evidence)

Recipe: _____

Source: _____
(who to blame)

_____   _____   _____   _____
Servings   Prep Time   Cooking Time   Temperature
               (triple this) (will probably take longer)

INGREDiENTS:

_____
_____
_____
_____
_____
_____
_____
_____
_____
_____
_____
_____
_____
_____
_____
_____
_____
_____
_____
_____
_____
_____
_____
_____
_____
_____
_____

Notes/Substitutions:

_____
_____
_____
_____

DiRectioNs: (if you choose to follow them)

About My MasterPiece:

(photographic evidence)

Recipe: _____

Source: _____
(who to blame)

_____   _____   _____   _____
Servings   Prep Time   Cooking Time   Temperature
                    (triple this)   (will probably take longer)

INGRedients:

_____
_____
_____
_____
_____
_____
_____
_____
_____
_____
_____
_____
_____
_____
_____
_____
_____
_____
_____
_____
_____
_____
_____
_____
_____
_____

Notes/Substitutions:

_____
_____
_____
_____

Directions: (if you choose to follow them)

About My Masterpiece:

(photographic evidence)

Recipe: _____

Source: _____
(who to blame)

_____ _____ _____ _____
Servings   Prep Time   Cooking Time   Temperature
                (triple this)   (will probably take longer)

INGREDIENTS:

_____
_____
_____
_____
_____
_____
_____
_____
_____
_____
_____
_____
_____
_____
_____
_____
_____
_____
_____
_____
_____
_____
_____
_____
_____
_____
_____
_____
_____

Notes/Substitutions:

_____
_____
_____
_____

Directions: (if you choose to follow them)

_____
_____
_____
_____
_____
_____
_____
_____
_____
_____
_____
_____
_____
_____

About My Masterpiece:

_____
_____
_____

(photographic evidence)

Recipe: _____

Source: _____
(who to blame)

_____   _____   _____   _____
Servings   Prep Time   Cooking Time   Temperature
                 (triple this)   (will probably take longer)

INGredients:

_____
_____
_____
_____
_____
_____
_____
_____
_____
_____
_____
_____
_____
_____
_____
_____
_____
_____
_____
_____
_____
_____
_____
_____
_____

Notes/Substitutions:

_____
_____
_____

DiRectioNs: (if you choose to follow them)

_____
_____
_____
_____
_____
_____
_____
_____
_____
_____
_____
_____
_____

About My Masterpiece:

_____
_____
_____

(photographic evidence)

Recipe: _____

Source: _____
(who to blame)

_____   _____   _____   _____
Servings   Prep Time   Cooking Time   Temperature
              (triple this) (will probably take longer)

INGReDieNTS:

_____
_____
_____
_____
_____
_____
_____
_____
_____
_____
_____
_____
_____
_____
_____
_____
_____
_____
_____
_____
_____
_____
_____
_____
_____
_____

Notes/Substitutions:

_____
_____
_____
_____

DIRECTIONS: (if you choose to follow them)

About My Masterpiece:

(photographic evidence)

Recipe: _____

Source: _____
(who to blame)

_____ _____ _____ _____
Servings   Prep Time   Cooking Time   Temperature
              (triple this)   (will probably take longer)

INGREDIENTS:

_____
_____
_____
_____
_____
_____
_____
_____
_____
_____
_____
_____
_____
_____
_____
_____
_____
_____
_____
_____
_____
_____
_____
_____
_____
_____

Notes/Substitutions:

_____
_____
_____
_____

DIRECTIONS: (if you choose to follow them)

About My Masterpiece:

(photographic evidence)

Recipe: _____

Source: _____
(who to blame)

_____ | _____ | _____ | _____
Servings | Prep Time | Cooking Time | Temperature
| (triple this) | (will probably take longer) |

INGREDIENTS:

_____
_____
_____
_____
_____
_____
_____
_____
_____
_____
_____
_____
_____
_____
_____
_____
_____
_____
_____
_____
_____
_____
_____
_____
_____
_____
_____

Notes/Substitutions:

_____
_____
_____
_____

Directions: (if you choose to follow them)

About My Masterpiece:

(photographic evidence)

Recipe: _____

Source: _____
(who to blame)

_____   _____   _____   _____
Servings   Prep Time   Cooking Time   Temperature
                  (triple this)   (will probably take longer)

INGReDients:

_____
_____
_____
_____
_____
_____
_____
_____
_____
_____
_____
_____
_____
_____
_____
_____
_____
_____
_____
_____
_____
_____
_____
_____

Notes/Substitutions:

_____
_____
_____

DirectioNS: (if you choose to follow them)

About My Masterpiece:

(photographic evidence)

Recipe: _____

Source: _____
(who to blame)

_____   _____   _____   _____
Servings   Prep Time   Cooking Time   Temperature
             (triple this) (will probably take longer)

INGREDIENTS:

_____
_____
_____
_____
_____
_____
_____
_____
_____
_____
_____
_____
_____
_____
_____
_____
_____
_____
_____
_____
_____
_____
_____
_____
_____
_____
_____

Notes/Substitutions:
_____
_____
_____
_____

DiRectioNS: (if you choose to follow them)

About My Masterpiece:

(photographic evidence)

Recipe: _____

Source: _____
(who to blame)

| Servings | Prep Time (triple this) | Cooking Time (will probably take longer) | Temperature |

INGREDIENTS:

_____
_____
_____
_____
_____
_____
_____
_____
_____
_____
_____
_____
_____
_____
_____
_____
_____
_____
_____
_____
_____
_____
_____
_____
_____
_____

Notes/Substitutions:

_____
_____
_____
_____

DiRectioNs: (if you choose to follow them)

About My Masterpiece:

(photographic evidence)

Recipe: _____

Source: _____
(who to blame)

Servings	Prep Time	Cooking Time	Temperature
	(triple this)	(will probably take longer)	

INGREDIENTS:

_____
_____
_____
_____
_____
_____
_____
_____
_____
_____
_____
_____
_____
_____
_____
_____
_____
_____
_____
_____
_____
_____
_____
_____
_____
_____
_____

Notes/Substitutions:

_____
_____
_____
_____

DiReCtioNS: (if you choose to follow them)

_____
_____
_____
_____
_____
_____
_____
_____
_____
_____
_____
_____
_____
_____
_____
_____
_____
_____

About My MasteRpiece:

_____
_____
_____
_____

(photographic evidence)

Recipe: _____

Source: _____
(who to blame)

_____   _____   _____   _____
Servings   Prep Time   Cooking Time   Temperature
                  (triple this)   (will probably take longer)

INGREDIENTS:

_____
_____
_____
_____
_____
_____
_____
_____
_____
_____
_____
_____
_____
_____
_____
_____
_____
_____
_____
_____
_____
_____
_____
_____
_____
_____
_____

Notes/Substitutions:

_____
_____
_____

DiRectioNS: (if you choose to follow them)

_____
_____
_____
_____
_____
_____
_____
_____
_____
_____
_____
_____
_____
_____
_____
_____

About My MasterPiece:

_____
_____
_____

(photographic evidence)

Recipe: _____

Source: _____
(who to blame)

_____ _____ _____ _____
Servings   Prep Time   Cooking Time   Temperature
           (triple this)   (will probably take longer)

INGREDIENTS:

_____
_____
_____
_____
_____
_____
_____
_____
_____
_____
_____
_____
_____
_____
_____
_____
_____
_____
_____
_____
_____
_____
_____
_____
_____
_____
_____
_____
_____

Notes/Substitutions:

_____
_____
_____
_____

DiRectioNs: (if you choose to follow them)

About My MasteRpiece:

(photographic evidence)

Recipe: _____

Source: _____
(who to blame)

_____ _____ _____ _____
Servings   Prep Time   Cooking Time   Temperature
           (triple this) (will probably take longer)

INGREDIENTS:

_____
_____
_____
_____
_____
_____
_____
_____
_____
_____
_____
_____
_____
_____
_____
_____
_____
_____
_____
_____
_____
_____
_____
_____
_____
_____

Notes/Substitutions:

_____
_____
_____
_____

DiRectioNS: (if you choose to follow them)

About My MasteRpiece:

(photogRaphic evidence)

Recipe: _____

Source: _____
(who to blame)

_____   _____   _____   _____
Servings   Prep Time   Cooking Time   Temperature
             (triple this)   (will probably take longer)

INGREDIENTS:

_____

_____

_____

_____

_____

_____

_____

_____

_____

_____

_____

_____

_____

_____

_____

_____

_____

_____

_____

_____

_____

_____

_____

_____

Notes/Substitutions:

_____

_____

_____

DiRectioNS: (if you choose to follow them)

_____
_____
_____
_____
_____
_____
_____
_____
_____
_____
_____
_____
_____
_____

About My Masterpiece:

_____
_____
_____
_____

(photographic evidence)

Recipe: _____

Source: _____
(who to blame)

_____   _____   _____   _____
Servings   Prep Time   Cooking Time   Temperature
            (triple this) (will probably take longer)

Ingredients:

_____
_____
_____
_____
_____
_____
_____
_____
_____
_____
_____
_____
_____
_____
_____
_____
_____
_____
_____
_____
_____
_____
_____
_____
_____
_____
_____
_____
_____
_____
_____

Notes/Substitutions:

_____
_____
_____
_____

DiRectioNs: (if you choose to follow them)

About My Masterpiece:

(photographic evidence)

Recipe: _____

Source: _____
(who to blame)

_____ | _____ | _____ | _____
Servings | Prep Time | Cooking Time | Temperature
| (triple this) | (will probably take longer) |

INGREDIENTS:

_____
_____
_____
_____
_____
_____
_____
_____
_____
_____
_____
_____
_____
_____
_____
_____
_____
_____
_____
_____
_____
_____
_____
_____
_____
_____
_____
_____

Notes/Substitutions:
_____
_____
_____

DiReCtioNS: (if you choose to follow them)

About My Masterpiece:

(photographic evidence)

Recipe: _____

Source: _____
(who to blame)

_____   _____   _____   _____
Servings   Prep Time   Cooking Time   Temperature
              (triple this)   (will probably take longer)

INGREDIENTS:

_____
_____
_____
_____
_____
_____
_____
_____
_____
_____
_____
_____
_____
_____
_____
_____
_____
_____
_____
_____
_____
_____
_____
_____

Notes/Substitutions:

_____
_____
_____

DiReCTioNS: (if you choose to follow them)

About My Masterpiece:

(photographic evidence)

Recipe: _____

Source: _____
(who to blame)

_____   _____   _____   _____
Servings   Prep Time   Cooking Time   Temperature
                 (triple this)   (will probably take longer)

INGREDIENTS:

_____
_____
_____
_____
_____
_____
_____
_____
_____
_____
_____
_____
_____
_____
_____
_____
_____
_____
_____
_____
_____
_____
_____
_____
_____
_____
_____
_____
_____

Notes/Substitutions:

_____
_____
_____
_____

DiReCTioNS: (if you choose to follow them)

About My Masterpiece:

(photographic evidence)

Recipe: _____

Source: _____
(who to blame)

_____ | _____ | _____ | _____
Servings | Prep Time | Cooking Time | Temperature
 | (triple this) | (will probably take longer) |

INGREDIENTS:

_____
_____
_____
_____
_____
_____
_____
_____
_____
_____
_____
_____
_____
_____
_____
_____
_____
_____
_____
_____
_____
_____
_____
_____
_____
_____
_____
_____
_____

Notes/Substitutions:

_____
_____
_____
_____

DiRectioNS: (if you choose to follow them)

about My MasterPiece:

(photographic evidence)

Recipe: _____

Source: _____
(who to blame)

_____	_____	_____	_____
Servings	Prep Time	Cooking Time	Temperature
	(triple this)	(will probably take longer)	

INGREDIENTS:

_____
_____
_____
_____
_____
_____
_____
_____
_____
_____
_____
_____
_____
_____
_____
_____
_____
_____
_____
_____
_____
_____
_____
_____
_____
_____
_____

Notes/Substitutions:

_____
_____
_____
_____

DiRectioNS: (if you choose to follow them)

About My Masterpiece:

(photographic evidence)

Recipe: _____

Source: _____
(who to blame)

_____ _____ _____ _____
Servings   Prep Time   Cooking Time   Temperature
             (triple this) (will probably take longer)

INGREDIENTS:

_____
_____
_____
_____
_____
_____
_____
_____
_____
_____
_____
_____
_____
_____
_____
_____
_____
_____
_____
_____
_____
_____
_____
_____
_____
_____
_____
_____
_____
_____
_____

Notes/Substitutions:

_____
_____
_____
_____

DiRectioNS: (if you choose to follow them)

About My MasteRpiece:

(photographic evidence)

Recipe: _____

Source: _____
(who to blame)

| Servings | Prep Time (triple this) | Cooking Time (will probably take longer) | Temperature |

INGREDIENTS:

_____
_____
_____
_____
_____
_____
_____
_____
_____
_____
_____
_____
_____
_____
_____
_____
_____
_____
_____
_____
_____
_____
_____
_____
_____
_____

Notes/Substitutions:

_____
_____
_____
_____

DiRectioNS: (if you choose to follow them)

_____
_____
_____
_____
_____
_____
_____
_____
_____
_____
_____
_____
_____
_____
_____
_____

About My Masterpiece:

_____
_____
_____

(photographic evidence)

Recipe: _____

Source: _____
(who to blame)

_____   _____   _____   _____
Servings   Prep Time   Cooking Time   Temperature
               (triple this)   (will probably take longer)

INGREDIENTS:

_____
_____
_____
_____
_____
_____
_____
_____
_____
_____
_____
_____
_____
_____
_____
_____
_____
_____
_____
_____
_____
_____
_____
_____
_____
_____
_____
_____

Notes/Substitutions:

_____
_____
_____
_____

DiRectioNs: (if you choose to follow them)

About My MasteRpiece:

(photographic evidence)

Recipe: _____

Source: _____
(who to blame)

| Servings | Prep Time (triple this) | Cooking Time (will probably take longer) | Temperature |

INGREDIENTS:

_____
_____
_____
_____
_____
_____
_____
_____
_____
_____
_____
_____
_____
_____
_____
_____
_____
_____
_____
_____
_____
_____
_____
_____
_____
_____
_____
_____
_____
_____

Notes/Substitutions:
_____
_____
_____
_____

DIRECTIONS: (if you choose to follow them)

About My Masterpiece:

(photographic evidence)

what I Learned

What I Still Need to Learn

Final Thoughts

(Creative new vocabulary invented, spells/curses performed)

Printed in Great Britain
by Amazon

72769678R00066